The Official CELTIC FOOTBALL CLUB Annual 2010

Written by Joe Sullivan & Gregor Kyle

A Grange Publication

© 2009. Published by Grange Communications Ltd., Edinburgh, under licence from Celtic Football Club. Printed in the EU.

Photographs © Alan Whyte, Angus Johnston, SNS Group & Press Association Images

Celtic logo is a registered trademark of The Celtic Football Club.

ISBN 978-1-906211-74-5

£6.99

CONTENTS

CLUB HONOURS

SCOTTISH LEAGUE WINNERS [42 TIMES]

1892/93, 1893/94, 1895/96, 1897/98, 1904/05, 1905/06, 1906/07, 1907/08, 1908/09, 1909/10, 1913/14, 1914/15, 1915/16, 1916/17, 1918/19, 1921/22, 1925/26, 1935/36, 1937/38, 1953/54, 1965/66, 1966/67, 1967/68, 1968/69, 1969/70, 1970/71, 1971/72, 1972/73, 1973/74, 1976/77, 1978/79, 1980/81, 1981/82, 1985/86, 1987/88, 1997/98, 2000/01, 2001/02, 2003/04, 2005/06, 2006/07, 2007/08

SCOTTISH CUP WINNERS [34 TIMES]

1892, 1899, 1900, 1904, 1907, 1908, 1911, 1912, 1914, 1923, 1925, 1927, 1931, 1933, 1937, 1951, 1954, 1965, 1967, 1969, 1971, 1972, 1974, 1975, 1977, 1980, 1985, 1988, 1989, 1995, 2001, 2004, 2005, 2007

LEAGUE CUP WINNERS [14 TIMES]

1956/57, 1957/58, 1965/66, 1966/67, 1967/68, 1968/69, 1969/70, 1974/75, 1982/83, 1997/98, 1999/00, 2000/01, 2005/06, 2008/09

EUROPEAN CUP WINNERS 1967

CORONATION CUP WINNERS 1953

TONY MOWBRAY

MANAGER FACTFILE

D.O.B: 22/09/63   **Born:** Saltburn

Playing career record:
Middlesbrough (1982-91), Celtic (1991-95),
Ipswich Town (1995-2000)

Playing honours:
Promotion from Division Three to Division Two
1986/87 / Promotion from Division Two to Division
One 1987/88 / Promotion to Premier League 1999/00

Managerial history:
Ipswich Town (caretaker, October 2002),
Hibernian (2004 -06),
West Bromwich Albion (2006-09)

Managerial honours:

Championship winners (2007/08)

Three England 'B' caps: Switzerland (A) 2-0,
Iceland (A) 2-0, Norway (A) 1-0 – all 1989

Scottish Football Writers' Manager of the Year
2005 – the only English winner of this award

MANY Celtic players have made their mark on the club thanks to their exploits on the field of play during the 90 minutes – only one has left a lasting legacy that raises the hairs on the backs of 60,000 necks even before a ball has been kicked in every single game at Paradise.

Tony Mowbray is that man and the Celt who started the world-famous Huddle returned to the club as manager at the start of this season when he took over from Gordon Strachan.

His credentials as a player, a manager and a Celt matched exactly what the club was looking for and, on June 17, 2009, Tony Mowbray walked through the hallowed portals of Paradise as the first English-born manager of the Hoops.

A Middlesbrough legend as a player, where he was tutored in the skills of the game by Lisbon Lion Bobby Murdoch, Tony Mowbray made an impressive debut as a Celt on November 9, 1991 when he cracked the woodwork from fully 35 yards as Celtic beat Aberdeen 2-1 in the East End of Glasgow.

That was the first of 103 Celtic games, 100 of them starts, during which he scored five goals and his leadership qualities on the park would translate to coaching and management attributes off the park with consummate ease as his time with his last club as a player, Ipswich Town, saw him edge into that sphere as interim manager.

A very successful stint as manager with Hibernian followed before he returned south to lead West Bromwich Albion where his continued success in producing attractive football caught the eyes of many – including those inside Celtic Park who saw him as the natural successor to carry on the work of Martin O'Neill and Gordon Strachan in bringing more success and silverware to Celtic Football Club.

SEASON REVIEW

JULY AUGUST

GOAL OF THE MONTH
Georgios Samaras' second v Falkirk

ENGLAND, Portugal and The Netherlands were on the agenda as Celtic kicked-off their pre-season itinerary of no fewer than eight warm-up games and Southampton (2-0) and Fulham (1-3) were first on the card before flying over for the Algarve Challenge Cup where Middlesbrough (1-1) and Cardiff City (0-1) awaited.

A 1-0 friendly win over Porto was also squeezed in while in Portugal and the next port of call was the Feyenoord Jubilee Tournament and games against Tottenham Hotspur (0-2) and Feyenoord (3-1).

Back home at Celtic Park, a 1-1 draw with Manchester City rounded off the preliminaries as the Hoops steadied themselves for the real thing when the league campaign kicked-off with the visit of St Mirren and a spot-kick from Barry Robson was enough to give the Celts a 1-0 win.

Paul Hartley was next on target in a 1-1 draw with Dundee United – a pattern that was to permeate the season when these teams met – and a 3-0 home win over Falkirk thanks to goals from Stephen McManus and Georgios Samaras (2) brought another three points.

August finished on a dull note when the Hoops played host to Rangers and lost 4-2 in the first derby meeting of the season.

ARCHIVE ACTION – August 23

WHILE the likes of Marc Crosas and Glenn Loovens made their debuts against Falkirk, the day also marked the 50th Anniversary of Celtic legend Billy McNeill's debut when the Hoops beat Clyde 2-0 in the League Cup in 1958. It was also exactly 25 years since Tommy Burns signed pro forms with the club.

SEPTEMBER

THANKS to the international break, the month was all but two weeks old before Celtic took part in their first action, but after that it was all hands on deck with no fewer than SIX matches crammed into the following fortnight.

First up was a trip to Fir Park and another Samaras double was added to by Scott McDonald and Shaun Maloney in a 4-2 win over Motherwell, while a week later another away trip to Kilmarnock yielded a 3-1 win with yet another Samaras double and a Maloney counter.

Both of those wins sandwiched Celtic's first Champions League encounter of the season when Danish side Aalborg visited but a 0-0 draw was the outcome.

ARCHIVE ACTION – September 27

THE 3-2 scoreline over Aberdeen may have been close but it wasn't as nail-biting as a game played on the same date 19 years earlier. That evening saw the Celts beat Partizan Belgrade 5-4 in the European Cup-Winners' Cup with Dariusz Dziekanowski scoring FOUR goals – but the Hoops still went out on the away-goals rule in 1989.

Next up was Co-operative Insurance Cup business and the Celts ensured their interest in the trophy with a 4-0 win over Livingston featuring, you've guessed it, a double from Samaras, and goals from Glenn Loovens and Scott Brown.

An exhilarating 3-2 win over Aberdeen was next on the cards with, this time, Jan Vennegoor of Hesselink netting twice, his second coming in the final minute and Scott McDonald heading the other goal.

September finished with another Champions League game and a trip to Spain but it ended in a 1-0 defeat to Villarreal.

GOAL OF THE MONTH
Shaun Maloney v Kilmarnock

FIRST Division champions Hamilton Accies were welcomed to open the month at Celtic Park and the Hoops dished out a 4-0 defeat to the Premier newcomers thanks to goals from Georgios Samaras, Scott McDonald, Aiden McGeady and Shunsuke Nakamura, while Glenn Loovens and Scott Brown were again on target in the next game as Inverness Caley Thistle lost 2-1 to the Celts up north.

The south was the next destination with Old Trafford beckoning in the Champions League, but a stylish Manchester United side won 3-0 on the night.

The Celts returned to Paradise with a 4-2 win over Hibernian with Cillian Sheridan netting his first Celtic goal while Stephen McManus, Loovens and Brown also got on the scoresheet.

GOAL OF THE MONTH
Aiden McGeady
v Kilmarnock

ARCHIVE ACTION – October 29

THE Celts played only their second League Cup game of the season when they beat Kilmarnock 3-1, but on the same day in 1966 they were playing their 10th of the tournament while beating Rangers 1-0 in the final to kick off the glorious 1966/67 clean sweep of all trophies.

The action for the month of October was finished with a trip to Rugby Park to take on Kilmarnock in the Co-operative Insurance Cup.

Scott McDonald opened the scoring with a header and when the Aussie was later fouled outside the box, Nakamura stepped up to double Celtic's lead with one of his trademark free kicks.

The best was saved 'til last though when, after Kilmarnock had pulled one back, a sublime move ended with a sweet shot from McGeady ending up in the back of the Killie net.

NOVEMBER

ARCHIVE ACTION – November 2

CELTIC kicked off the month with a 2-0 win over Hearts, while on the same day 14 years earlier Tosh McKinlay kicked off his Hoops career after signing from the Tynecastle club in 1994 and he went on to have a magnificent five seasons with his Bhoyhood heroes.

THIS was by far the busiest month of the season with eight games crammed in and plenty of action too with the sequence kicking off with a 2-0 win at Tynecastle against Hearts as a stunner from Shaun Maloney and a back-post knock-over from Gary Caldwell sealed a 2-0 win.

Next up were Manchester United and an exquisite lob from Scott McDonald put Celtic in the lead after 12 minutes, but the Hoops' hopes were dashed just five minutes from the end when Ryan Giggs latched on to an Artur Boruc parry from a Cristiano Ronaldo shot to cruelly level the game.

There then followed a string of domestic victories broken only by a 2-1 away Champions League defeat to Aalborg in the second-last game of the month.

Motherwell and Kilmarnock were beaten 2-0 and 3-0 respectively in a four-day double-header at Celtic Park.

Celtic's first ever visit to New Douglas Park and their last ever visit to the old St Mirren Park came in consecutive games and yielded a 2-1 win over Hamilton Accies and a 3-1 win in Paisley just prior to the visit to Denmark.

The Hoops returned from Champions League duty to record a 1-0 home win over Inverness Caley Thistle thanks to a Shaun Maloney goal.

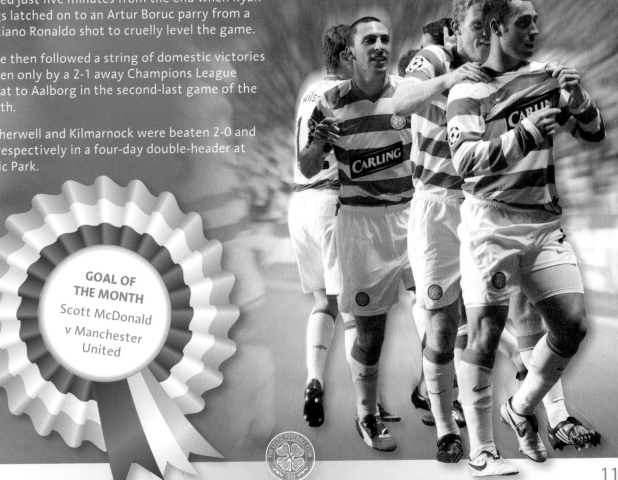

GOAL OF THE MONTH
Scott McDonald
v Manchester
United

11

DECEMBER

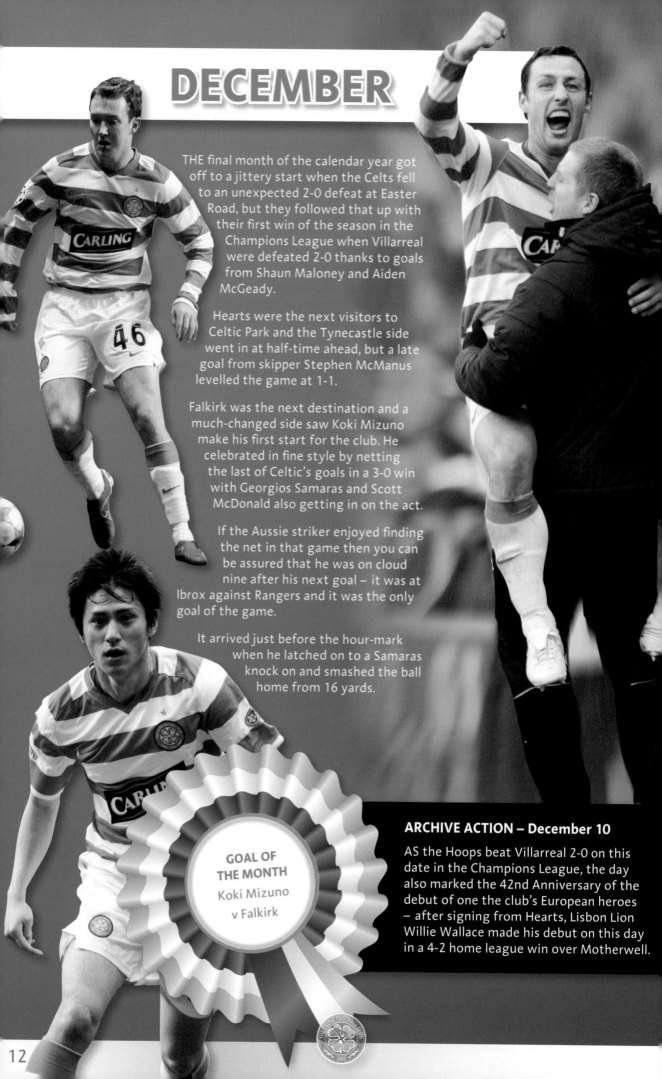

THE final month of the calendar year got off to a jittery start when the Celts fell to an unexpected 2-0 defeat at Easter Road, but they followed that up with their first win of the season in the Champions League when Villarreal were defeated 2-0 thanks to goals from Shaun Maloney and Aiden McGeady.

Hearts were the next visitors to Celtic Park and the Tynecastle side went in at half-time ahead, but a late goal from skipper Stephen McManus levelled the game at 1-1.

Falkirk was the next destination and a much-changed side saw Koki Mizuno make his first start for the club. He celebrated in fine style by netting the last of Celtic's goals in a 3-0 win with Georgios Samaras and Scott McDonald also getting in on the act.

If the Aussie striker enjoyed finding the net in that game then you can be assured that he was on cloud nine after his next goal – it was at Ibrox against Rangers and it was the only goal of the game.

It arrived just before the hour-mark when he latched on to a Samaras knock on and smashed the ball home from 16 yards.

GOAL OF THE MONTH
Koki Mizuno
v Falkirk

ARCHIVE ACTION – December 10

AS the Hoops beat Villarreal 2-0 on this date in the Champions League, the day also marked the 42nd Anniversary of the debut of one the club's European heroes – after signing from Hearts, Lisbon Lion Willie Wallace made his debut on this day in a 4-2 home league win over Motherwell.

JANUARY

THE New Year arrived and Dundee United were the first-footers. Georgios Samaras hit his fifth double of the season to put the Celts 2-0 ahead, but the visitors pulled two goals back to level the game.

The city of Dundee also provided the next visitors to Celtic Park but this time it was the Dens Park side on Scottish Cup duty, and they took a surprise lead before goals from Scott Brown and Aiden McGeady took the Hoops into the next round.

A trip to Aberdeen proved to be a real stumbling block with a shock 4-2 defeat stopping Celtic in their tracks, but

ARCHIVE ACTION –January 28

WHILE Artur Boruc was the League Cup penalty shoot-out hero of the night against Dundee United by both saving AND scoring kicks, the day marked what would have been legendary Celtic keeper John Thomson's 90th Birthday – he was born in Fife in 1909.

they followed that up with a 3-1 home win over Hibernian with two goals from Scott McDonald sandwiching a Stephen McManus effort.

A game against Dundee United also ended the month, and Hampden was the venue for an unforgettable penalty shoot-out epic as the teams were still tied 0-0 after extra-time and it went all the way to sudden death. Artur Boruc even scored, before Scott McDonald's deciding penalty made it 11-10 to Celtic.

GOAL OF THE MONTH
Artur Boruc
v Dundee
United

13

FEBRUARY

GOAL OF THE MONTH
Marc Crosas
v St Mirren

ARCHIVE ACTION – February 15

AS the Hoops drew 0-0 with Rangers on this day they could have done with some of the goalscoring enterprise of the 1897 Celts who found themselves 4-1 down to Arsenal, then known as Woolwich Arsenal, in an away friendly – the Bhoys rallied to score four second-half goals and win 5-4.

INVERNESS was the first port of call at the start of the new month, but Celtic returned from the Highlands with only one point after a 0-0 draw and readied themselves for the visit of Glasgow neighbours Queen's Park in the Scottish Cup.

Gary Caldwell and Scott McDonald gave the Hoops a 2-0 half-time lead, and although the Spiders pulled one back midway through the second 45, the Celts went through to the next round with a 2-1 victory.

A week later there was another rather more pressing Glasgow derby when Rangers visited on league duty but a 0-0 draw was the outcome, and the Celts had to settle for another single point the following weekend when they travelled to Fir Park with Scott McDonald netting in a 1-1 draw.

If goals were scarce during February then the Celts certainly rediscovered the road to the net in the final game of the month when St Mirren came calling.

The Hoops hammered the Buddies 7-0 with Shunsuke Nakamura setting the ball rolling before adding a second and netting his hat-trick on the hour-mark.

In between time, Marc Crosas and Scott Brown had also found the net meaning Nakamura's third had made it 5-0.

Brown added another and an own-goal made it 7-0 as the Celts celebrated their highest-scoring game of the season.

MARCH

A DOUBLE from Scott McDonald secured all three points as a 2-1 win at Rugby Park opened the month before more Scottish Cup action arrived in the shape of a visit to Paisley to take on St Mirren.

With the 7-0 demolition job still very much fresh in the memory, the home side shut up shop and a penalty strike gave them a shock 1-0 win just a week before Celtic would take part in more cup action with the Co-operative Insurance Cup final on the immediate horizon.

Rangers provided the opposition and despite Celtic taking the initiative, the 90 minutes finished goal-less but the 30 minutes of extra-time were bookended with Celtic goals.

The first came from Darren O'Dea when he headed home a Shunsuke Nakamura free kick and in the final minute, his Republic of Ireland international team-mate, Aiden McGeady was brought down after a surging run into the box.

McGeady dusted himself down and took the spot-kick himself to make it 2-0, and the League Cup was heading to Celtic Park for the 14th time.

The month finished with another drawn game against Dundee United, but this time it was the Celts who equalised late on in the game with Lee Naylor scoring a cracker to make it 2-2 after Scott McDonald had opened the scoring in the first half.

GOAL OF THE MONTH
Darren O'Dea
v Rangers

ARCHIVE ACTION – March 4

WHILE the Celts recorded their 2-1 away win over Kilmarnock, club legend Kenny Dalglish was celebrating his 58th birthday, as the man who would go on to score 167 goals in 320 Hoops games was born on this day just down the road from Celtic Park in Dalmarnock in 1951.

The co-operative insurance cup

Winners 2009

The co-operative insurance cup

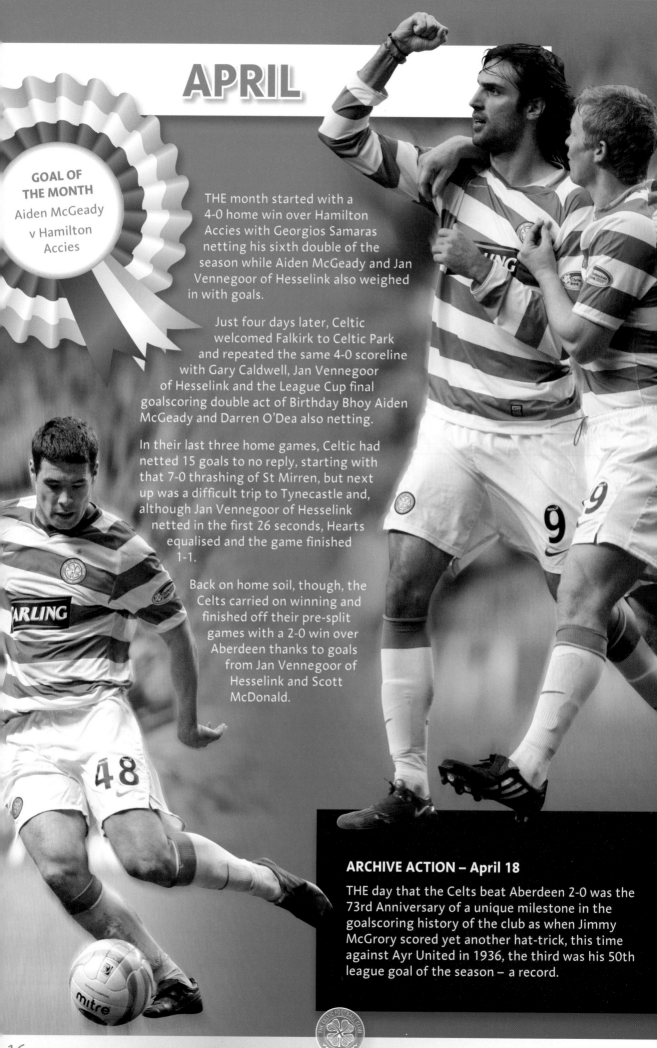

APRIL

GOAL OF THE MONTH
Aiden McGeady
v Hamilton Accies

THE month started with a 4-0 home win over Hamilton Accies with Georgios Samaras netting his sixth double of the season while Aiden McGeady and Jan Vennegoor of Hesselink also weighed in with goals.

Just four days later, Celtic welcomed Falkirk to Celtic Park and repeated the same 4-0 scoreline with Gary Caldwell, Jan Vennegoor of Hesselink and the League Cup final goalscoring double act of Birthday Bhoy Aiden McGeady and Darren O'Dea also netting.

In their last three home games, Celtic had netted 15 goals to no reply, starting with that 7-0 thrashing of St Mirren, but next up was a difficult trip to Tynecastle and, although Jan Vennegoor of Hesselink netted in the first 26 seconds, Hearts equalised and the game finished 1-1.

Back on home soil, though, the Celts carried on winning and finished off their pre-split games with a 2-0 win over Aberdeen thanks to goals from Jan Vennegoor of Hesselink and Scott McDonald.

ARCHIVE ACTION – April 18

THE day that the Celts beat Aberdeen 2-0 was the 73rd Anniversary of a unique milestone in the goalscoring history of the club as when Jimmy McGrory scored yet another hat-trick, this time against Ayr United in 1936, the third was his 50th league goal of the season – a record.

MAY

ARCHIVE ACTION – May 2

THE Hoops opened the month with a 3-1 win over Aberdeen exactly 108 years after the club's first visit to Ibrox on league duty when they came away with a 2-1 win with Johnny Madden and Peter Dowds scoring the goals in the very first Scottish League campaign in season 1890/91.

CELTIC'S last opponents of the previous month, their final opposition of the pre-split games, turned out to be their first rivals of the new month and, therefore, the first in the post-split games as the Hoops played back-to-back matches against Aberdeen.

This game was played at the tough venue of Pittodrie and things looked bleak when the home side took the lead, but Gary Caldwell equalised and Scott McDonald netted another double as the Celts ran out 3-1 winners.

Next up was a visit to Ibrox but a 1-0 defeat was the outcome, although the Hoops regained some ground with a 2-1 home win over Dundee United with Glenn Loovens and Georgios Samaras scoring the goals.

The ground was gained because Rangers drew 1-1 with Hibernian at Easter Road but four days later, the Celts drew 0-0 at the same venue meaning that everything hinged on the last day.

Celtic needed Rangers to lose at Tannadice while they themselves had to beat Hearts on the final day, but neither result arose as the Hoops finished the season with a 0-0 draw against Hearts.

HOOPS'

HOTSPOTS

IN the summer, as you enjoy your school holidays, the Celtic players will be looking forward to putting their feet up in the close-season break.

There is hardly time for anything other than the odd day-off during the league campaign, with games in Europe and Scotland and international matches making for a packed schedule which continues to the end of May.

Pre-season training, where the players do most of the fitness work that gets them in shape for the year ahead, starts in July, leaving June as the only month where they can enjoy a holiday.

Some will spend the time with their families and friends, while others fly out to foreign countries. Here we look at a few of their favourite destinations.

ANDREAS HINKEL

First: My parents weren't very rich and it was too expensive to go abroad, but we went camping in Germany every year until I was about 15. It was great because it was a great place for children and I played football, table tennis and mini golf with all the other kids.

Best: There are two kinds of holiday - adventure and relaxing - and I love them both. I have found a good place in the south of Spain called Chiclana and I really love going there.

Most Recent: I got to go home and see my family during the international break, but the last big holiday I had was Mexico in 2006 and I went to see the Mayan ruins, which was a great experience.

SCOTT McDONALD

First: Because Australia is such a big place we didn't used to leave the country. We went up to the Gold Coast every year and I enjoyed going to places like Movieworld and Seaworld. The weather was always great and the beaches are beautiful.

Best: I've been lucky enough to have a few good ones. Thailand was really amazing and I went to an island called Koh Samui, which was a great experience and totally different to anywhere else in the world. But I think my favourite is Dubai – which is the place to be right now.

Most Recent: My last holiday was in Dubai and it has made a lasting impression. The buildings are absolutely spectacular, the weather amazing and the service first class. I'll definitely be going back.

GARY CALDWELL

First: My first holiday was with my Mum and Dad and my brother Stephen on the Costa Del Sol. I loved swimming on holiday and we were always in the water, at the pool or on the beach.

Best: I love going anywhere in America. I have been to a few places and went to Florida recently. But I also love New York and Las Vegas. I love the food, the people and there is lots to do.

Most Recent: I was in Dubai on holiday and it was brilliant. It has everything, and everything that they do is bigger and better than anywhere else in the world. The service is amazing, people really look after you and it's a fantastic place.

MARC CROSAS

First: I lived in a great place called Girona, which has the Costa Brava and its beaches, so I stayed at home in the summer with my friends and family. I didn't go to other countries and it was nice for us, because a lot of tourists would come in and it helped us improve our English and our French.

Best: My favourite place to go on holiday, now that I live in Glasgow, is home. I love to go home and see everyone and spend all day at the beach. I just enjoy the good weather, but every summer I also go for a week or a few days to Ibiza.

Most Recent: I went to Brazil last June with my team-mate Fred from Lyon and stayed with his family for 15 days. It was very good, a great place to go on holiday.

For the second part of Hoops' Holiday Hotspots turn to pages 48/49 for more of your Celtic heroes' holiday destinations.

WHILE you might look to the current Celtic team as your football heroes, the players have their own favourites.

Whether they were growing up in Scotland, Ireland, Australia, Japan or Greece, they all imitated their idols in the playground and in matches, trying to copy and emulate their moves.

Little has changed since they have become professional footballers themselves, and here some of the first team talk about the players they used to, and still love to, watch.

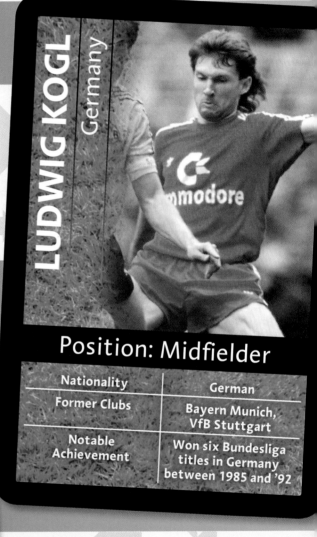

LUDWIG KOGL
Germany

ANDREAS HINKEL

"I had a few favourite players growing up. I was a Stuttgart fan and my hero was Ludwig Kogl. He was very similar to another of my favourite players, Pierre Littbarski, small, but strong and hard working and very technical, he was also a left footer. For a while it was Lothar Matthaus as well and later on it was Lillian Thuram, but when I was young I liked watching Ludwig Kogl."

Position: Midfielder

Nationality	German
Former Clubs	Bayern Munich, VfB Stuttgart
Notable Achievement	Won six Bundesliga titles in Germany between 1985 and '92

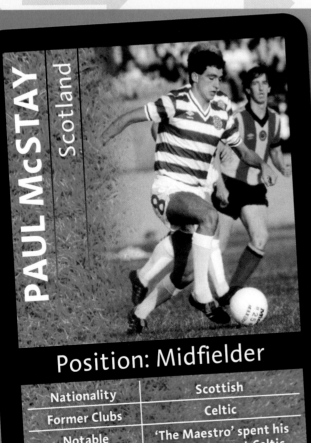

PAUL McSTAY
Scotland

Position: Midfielder

Nationality	Scottish
Former Clubs	Celtic
Notable Achievement	'The Maestro' spent his whole career at Celtic and was voted one of the Greatest Ever Celts by the supporters

SCOTT McDONALD

"I had two favourite players that Celtic supporters will remember well. One was Paolo Di Canio, who was a massive influence on me from the minute he joined the club. The other was Paul McStay, who was the club captain, a great Celtic player and my idol. He wore his heart on his sleeve and loved the club as well. There were a few others internationally, one was Romario, because he was small in stature, but strong, quick and a great finisher."

GLENN LOOVENS

"I always looked at defenders and how they were playing, because I have always been a defender. My favourite was Jaap Stam because of his physical power and he never got beaten. He was someone I always looked up to. I was a Feyenoord fan growing up and my foreign club was Barcelona, because they had a lot of Dutch players and I liked the way they played, but my favourite player was Jaap Stam."

JAAP STAM
Netherlands

Position: Centre half

Nationality	Dutch
Former Clubs	PSV, Manchester United, Lazio, AC Milan, Ajax
Notable Achievement	Won three league titles, the FA Cup, the Intercontinental Cup and Champions League in three years at Man United.

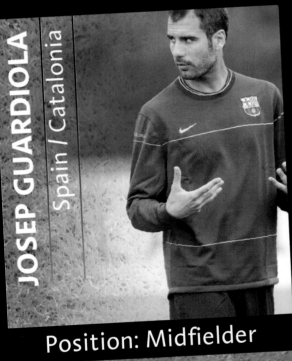

JOSEP GUARDIOLA
Spain / Catalonia

Position: Midfielder

Nationality	Spanish/Catalan
Former Clubs	Barcelona
Notable Achievement	Has won the Champions League (or European Cup) as a player and coach with Barcelona.

MARC CROSAS

"My favourite player was Josep Guardiola. I played for the youth teams at Barcelona and he played in the same position and was like a mirror for me. I wanted to play like him and I tried to learn from his style and how he played. Later on I had the chance to work with him in the second team and then, at the start of last season, I worked with him in pre-season with Barcelona, before I moved to Celtic. He was an amazing coach, like he was an amazing player, and he was great to work with."

For the second part of Your Favourites' Favourites turn to pages 58/59 for more heroes of the Celts.

PUZZLE PAGES

SPOT THE DIFFERENCE

There are 12 differences between these pictures of Scott McDonald weaving his way through the Hamilton Accies defence. The first one has been circled, but can you spot the rest?

Answers on pages 62/63.

SPL SEASON 2008/09 QUIZ

01 Which two players took to the field for the first time as Celts against Falkirk in August 2008?

02 And why was the same game special for Shaun Maloney?

03 Which Celt made his debut against Rangers in February 2009?

04 Which two SPL grounds did Celtic play on for the first time during the season?

05 Celtic's highest-scoring game was against which club?

06 Can you name the Celts who were out on loan at other SPL clubs during the season?

07 Which Celts made the most SPL appearances during the term?

08 And what player made only one appearance?

09 How many SPL games had Celtic played before they failed to find the net?

10 What was John Potter's claim to Celtic fame during the season?

How did you do? Find out with the answers on pages 62/63.

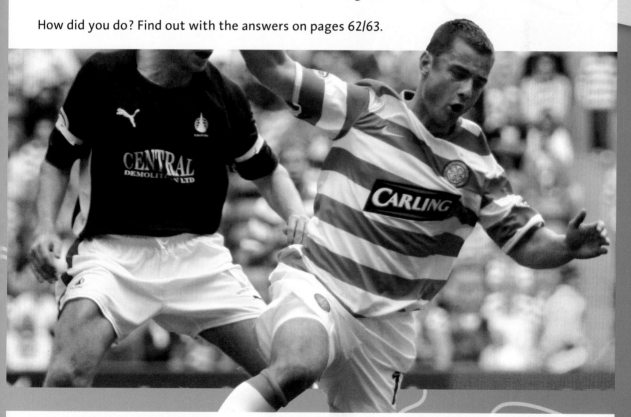

DID YOU KNOW?

There are 42 clubs playing senior football in Scotland, and of the other 41 there are three teams that Celtic have yet to meet in any of the three domestic competitions. The clubs are Airdrie United, Peterhead and Annan Athletic – although the Hoops did play the old Airdrie 163 times.

CELTIC SOCCER SKOOL

BECOMING the best you can be isn't all about practice, although that is obviously a major part of your football education. A crucial factor is listening to those who have been there and done it - they are the best teachers of all.

And at Celtic Park there is no shortage of words of wisdom from current players and Hoops legends of the past alike.

So your Celtic Annual got out there and asked some of the best experts around just what advice they would give to any youngster who wants to play for the Hoops.

GARY CALDWELL

MY advice to any young player who wants to make it as a professional footballer would be to work as hard as you can and, even if you have setbacks, keep coming back and working hard. A lot of it has to do with ability and how hard you work, but you have to be mentally strong as well. Listen to your coaches, your managers and your parents, listen to good advice, because plenty of people will give their opinions, but you should always listen to the people who matter and want what is best for you.

AIDEN McGEADY

THE best advice I can give to a young player is practice. If you have a love for the game, every time you have a spare five or 10 minutes, get out and practise, because that's what makes you a footballer. When I was younger all I wanted to do was play football and become a footballer and practice helps you get there. By practising, you hone your game and it helps you improve the little things, like working on both feet and improving your crossing and finishing. If you want to become a professional footballer, that's the way to do it.

DAVIE HAY

I THINK this would apply to any young footballer whether they're at Celtic or not, but the first thing for any youngster is practice. Keep practising and work as hard as you can. And if a setback comes, which can happen, have the mental strength to overcome it.

TOSH McKINLAY

MY advice to any young player would be to work hard and listen to every piece of advice that your coaches give you. They are only doing it for your good and their advice will stand you in good stead. You can catch the coach's eye by working hard and showing that you are listening to what they are saying – that 10 or 15 per cent of extra work in training could be the difference. During your career you see so many people falling by the wayside, people who perhaps had more talent than yourself, but were a bit lazy, didn't listen and then, all of a sudden, found themselves out of the game.

PETER GRANT

I WOULD tell any aspiring young player to give it their maximum. People say practice makes perfection, but for me it's perfect practice makes perfection. You have a lot of spare time on your hands so use it wisely, learn the game because the game is played with your mind. Understand what's asked of you and don't just do your two hours of training and then go and play the PlayStation. It's easy to do that nowadays, but young players should take the time to learn and improve. It's the best job in the world bar none and if the dream doesn't take you to being a Celtic regular, it will take you somewhere else and it's still a fantastic feeling to play no matter where you are. There's no better feeling than waking up and knowing that you have a game or training. It's the best feeling in the world and best job in the world, so don't waste your time or throw it away, grab it with both hands and give it your maximum.

FOR the second part of the Celtic Soccer Skool turn to pages 42/43 for more handy hints from those who passed with flying colours.

MAZE

Aiden McGeady has just finished a rigorous training session at Lennoxtown during which he found the road to goal quite easy.

But he now has to get down to Celtic Park for a signing session at the Superstore. Can you help get him there?

Find out how Aiden gets back to Paradise on pages 62/63.

QUIZ QUESTIONS

01 From which club did Celtic sign Willo Flood?

02 Which team did Celtic play in their opening round of the Co-operative Insurance Cup in September 2008?

03 And what was the score in the semi-final against Dundee United in January 2009?

04 How many different nationalities played for Celtic during the 2008/09 season?

05 Prior to season 2008/09, when was the last time Celtic played Hamilton Accies in the league?

Check out the answers on pages 62/63.

WORDSEARCH

01 The man who was Celtic's top striker in season 2008/09.

02 The club's old training ground.

03 The sort of games you get a cap for.

04 The land of Koki Mizuno.

05 These cats roared in Lisbon.

06 The first Celtic manager not to play for the club.

07 Old floodlights used to sit at the top of these.

08 Horizontal stripes.

09 Celtic have won this trophy 14 times.

Answers on pages 62/63.

K	R	N	N	Y	K	R	M	C	E	Z	B	C
S	C	O	T	T	M	C	D	O	N	A	L	D
O	N	A	R	E	V	N	I	K	R	D	S	L
U	A	L	R	B	T	D	J	R	F	N	T	Y
P	P	P	N	A	A	S	O	T	O	N	X	D
U	A	L	B	N	D	W	K	L	K	H	O	A
C	J	X	L	T	F	I	Y	C	K	L	N	R
E	L	A	G	I	R	P	S	X	O	J	N	B
U	T	Z	E	R	O	N	C	E	H	J	E	M
G	T	L	J	T	W	N	L	Y	V	Y	L	A
A	D	N	O	I	P	M	S	H	C	T	L	I
E	P	U	C	N	A	E	S	P	O	O	H	L
L	A	N	O	I	T	A	N	R	E	T	N	I

DID YOU KNOW?

Pat Bonner is the keeper who has made the most appearances for Celtic with 641 games amounting to over 57,690 minutes and that doesn't include time added on, extra-time or friendlies – so he has played over 1,000 hours for Celtic.

At the other end of the scale is Barry John Corr who replaced the injured Jonathan Gould in goal against Hearts in April, 1999 and played only 48 minutes for Celtic.

Artur Boruc
Position: Goalkeeper
Squad Number: 1
D.O.B: 20/02/1980
Born: Siedlce, Poland
Height: 6'4"
Signed: 14/07/05 (loan)
17/10/05 (signed)
Debut: v Artmedia
Bratislava (h) 4-0 (UCL)
02/08/05
Previous Clubs:
Legia Warsaw,
Dolcan Zabki (loan),
Pogon Siedlce

Lee Naylor
Position: Left-back
Squad Number: 3
D.O.B: 19/03/1980
Born: Walsall, England
Height: 5'10"
Signed: 25/08/06
Debut: v Hibernian (h) 2-1
(SPL) 26/08/06
Previous Clubs:
Wolverhampton
Wanderers

Gary Caldwell
Position: Centre-back
Squad Number: 5
D.O.B: 12/04/82
Born: Stirling, Scotland
Height: 5'11"
Signed: 01/06/06
Debut: v Kilmarnock
(h) 4-1 (SPL) 29/07/06
Previous Clubs:
Hibernian,
Derby County (loan),
Coventry City (loan),
Hibernian (loan),
Darlington (loan),
Newcastle United

Player Profiles

Andreas Hinkel
Position: Right-back
Squad Number: 2
D.O.B: 26/03/82
Born: Backnang, Germany
Height: 6'0"
Signed: 04/01/08
Debut: v Stirling Albion (h)
3-1 (SC) 12/01/08
Previous Clubs:
Sevilla,
VfB Stuttgart

Scott Brown
Position: Midfielder
Squad Number: 8
D.O.B: 25/06/85
Born: Hill o' Beath,
Scotland
Height: 5'10"
Signed: 01/07/07
Debut: v Kilmarnock (h)
0-0 (SPL) 05/08/07
Previous Clubs: Hibernian

Barry Robson
Position: Midfielder
Squad Number: 19
D.O.B: 07/11/78
Born: Aberdeen, Scotland
Height: 6'0"
Signed: 31/01/08
Debut: v Aberdeen (a) 5-1
(SPL) 10/02/08
Previous Clubs:
Dundee United,
Forfar Athletic (loan),
Inverness CT,
Rangers

Player Profiles

Koki Mizuno
Position: Winger
Squad Number: 29
D.O.B: 06/09/85
Born: Shimiz-Ku, Japan
Height: 5'8"
Signed: 31/01/08
Debut: v Falkirk (a) 3-0
(SPL) 21/12/08
Previous Clubs:
JEF United

Shaun Maloney
Position: Midfielder
Squad Number: 13
Date of Birth: 24/01/83
Born: Sarawak, Malaysia
Height: 5'7"
Signed: 22/08/08
Debut: v Falkirk (h) 3-0
(SPL) 23/08/08
Former clubs:
Aston Villa,
Celtic Youth

Massimo Donati
Position: Midfielder
Squad Number: 18
D.O.B: 26/03/81
Born: Sedegliano, Italy
Height: 6'1"
Signed: 29/06/07
Debut: v Kilmarnock (h)
0-0 (SPL) 05/08/07
Previous Clubs:
AC Milan,
Atalanta (loan),
Messina (loan),
Sampdoria (loan),
Torino (loan),
Parma (loan)

Player Profiles

Marc Crosas
Position: Midfielder
Squad Number: 17
D.O.B: 09/01/88
Born: Girona, Spain
Height: 5'8"
Signed: 01/08/08
Debut: v Falkirk (h) 3-0 (SPL) 23/08/08
Previous Clubs: Lyon (loan), Barcelona

Willo Flood
Position: Midfielder
Squad Number: 16
D.O.B: 10/04/85
Born: Dublin, Ireland
Height: 5'6"
Signed: 30/01/09
Debut: v Rangers (h) 0-0 (SPL) 14/03/09
Previous Clubs: Dundee United (loan), Cardiff City, Rochdale (loan), Coventry City (loan), Manchester City.

Cillian Sheridan
Position: Centre-forward
Squad Number: 26
D.O.B: 23/02/89
Born: Cavan, Ireland
Height: 6'2"
Signed: 10/02/06
Debut: v Inverness (a) 2-1 (SC) 25/02/07
Previous Clubs: Motherwell (loan), Celtic Youth

Player Profiles

Scott McDonald
Position: **Centre-forward**
Squad Number: **7**
D.O.B: **21/08/83**
Born: **Melbourne, Australia**
Height: **5'8"**
Signed: **01/07/07**
Debut: **v Spartak Moscow (a) 1-1 (UCL) 15/08/07**
Previous Clubs: **Motherwell, Milton Keynes Dons (loan), Bournemouth (loan), Huddersfield (loan), Southampton**

Ben Hutchinson
Position: **Centre-forward**
Squad Number: **23**
D.O.B: **27/11/87**
Born: **Nottingham, England**
Height: **5'11"**
Signed: **31/01/08**
Debut: **v Hearts (h) 3-0 (SPL) 16/02/08**
Previous Clubs: **Middlesbrough**

Chris Killen
Position: **Striker**
Squad Number: **33**
D.O.B: **08/10/81**
Born: **Wellington, New Zealand**
Height: **6'0"**
Signed:**02/06/07**
Debut: **v Kilmarnock (h) 0-0 (SPL) 05/08/07**
Previous Clubs: **Hibernian, Oldham, Port Vale (loan), Wrexham (loan), Man City**

Player Profiles

John Kennedy
Position: Centre-back
Squad Number: 41
D.O.B: 18/08/83
Born: Bellshill, Scotland
Height: 6'2"
Signed: 20/08/99
Debut: v Motherwell (h)
4-0 (SPL) 05/04/2000
Previous Clubs:
Norwich (loan),
Celtic Youth

Stephen McManus
Position: Centre-back
Squad Number: 4
D.O.B: 10/09/82
Born: Lanark, Scotland
Height: 6'2"
Signed: 20/08/99
Debut: v Hibernian (a) 4-0
(SPL) 21/03/04
Previous Clubs:
Celtic Youth

Aiden McGeady
Position: Midfielder
Squad Number: 46
D.O.B: 04/04/86
Born: Glasgow, Scotland
Height: 5'10"
Signed: 20/07/02
Debut: v Hearts (a) 1-1
(SPL) 25/04/04
Previous Clubs:
Celtic Youth

Player Profiles

Darren O'Dea
Position: Defender
Squad Number: 48
D.O.B: 04/02/87
Born: Dublin, Ireland
Height: 6'1"
Signed: 01/08/05
Debut: v St Mirren (h) 2-0
(SLC) 19/09/06
Previous Clubs:
Celtic Youth

Georgios Samaras
Position: Centre-forward
Squad Number: 9
D.O.B: 21/02/85
Born: Heraklion, Greece
Height: 6'4"
Signed: 29/01/08
Debut: v Kilmarnock (a)
5-1 (SC) 02/02/08
Previous Clubs:
Manchester City,
Heerenveen

Paul Caddis
Position: Right-back
Squad Number: 52
D.O.B: 19/04/88
Born: Irvine, Scotland
Height: 5'7"
Signed: 01/07/04
Debut: v Falkirk (a) 1-0
(SC) 27/01/08
Previous Clubs:
Dundee United (loan),
Celtic Youth

Player Profiles

Lukasz Zaluska
Position: Goalkeeper
Squad Number: 24
D.O.B: 16/06/82
Born: Wysokie
Mazowieckie, Poland
Height: 6'4"
Signed: 01/06/09
Debut: N/A
Previous Clubs:
Dundee United,
Korona Kielce,
Legia Warsaw,
Stomil Olsztyn,
Zryw Zielona Gora,
Sparta Obornoki,
MSP Szamotuly,
Ruch Wysokie
Mazowieckie

Glenn Loovens
Position: Centre-back
Squad Number: 22
D.O.B: 22/10/83
Born: Doetinchem,
Netherlands
Height: 5'10"
Signed: 16/08/08
Debut: v Falkirk (h) 3-0
(SPL) 23/08/08
Previous Clubs:
Cardiff City,
De Graafschap (loan),
Excelsior (loan),
Feyenoord

Mark Wilson
Position: Full-back
Squad Number: 12
D.O.B: 05/06/84
Born: Glasgow, Scotland
Height: 5'10"
Signed: 16/01/06
Debut: v Dundee United
(h) 3-3 (SPL) 28/01/06
Previous Clubs:
Dundee United

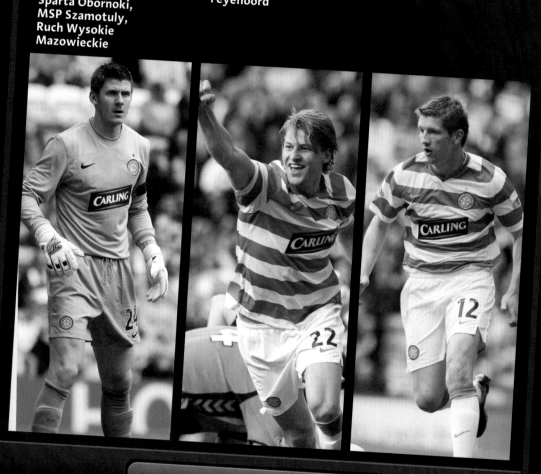

Player Profiles

Landry N'Guemo
Position: Midfielder
Squad Number: 6
Date of Birth: 28/11/85
Born: Yaoundé, Cameroon
Height: 5'8"
Signed: 16/07/09
Debut: v Dinamo Moscow
(h) 0-1 (UCL) 29/07/09
Former clubs:
AS Nancy

Marc-Antoine Fortune
Position: Centre-forward
Squad Number: 10
Date of Birth: 02/07/81
Born: Cayenne,
French Guiana
Height: 6'0"
Signed: 09/07/09
Debut: v Dinamo Moscow
(h) 0-1 (UCL) 29/07/09
Previous Clubs:
West Bromwich
Albion (loan),
AS Nancy,
Utrecht,
Stade Brest,
Rouen (loan),
Lille,
Angouleme

Danny Fox
Position: Left-back
Squad Number: 11
Date of Birth: 29/05/86
Born: Winsford, England
Height: 6'0"
Signed: 24/07/09
Debut: v Dinamo Moscow
(h) 0-1 (UCL) 29/07/09
Former clubs:
Coventry City,
Walsall,
Stranraer (loan),
Everton

Player Profiles

DATE	TEAM	
15/08/09	Aberdeen	A
22/08/09	St Johnstone	H
30/08/09	Hibernian	A
12/09/09	Dundee United	H
19/09/09	Hearts	H
26/09/09	St Mirren	A
04/10/09	Rangers	A
17/10/09	Motherwell	H
24/10/09	Hamilton Accies	A
31/10/09	Kilmarnock	H
07/11/09	Falkirk	A
21/11/09	Dundee United	A
28/11/09	St Mirren	H
05/12/09	Aberdeen	H
12/12/09	Motherwell	A
19/12/09	Hearts	A
26/12/09	Hamilton Accies	H
30/12/09	Kilmarnock	A
02/01/10	Rangers	H
16/01/10	Falkirk	H
23/01/10	St Johnstone	A
27/01/10	Hibernian	H
30/01/10	Hamilton Accies	A
10/02/10	Hearts	H
13/02/10	Aberdeen	A
20/02/10	Dundee United	H
27/02/10	Rangers	A
06/03/10	Falkirk	A
20/03/10	St Johnstone	H
24/03/10	St Mirren	A
27/03/10	Kilmarnock	H
03/04/10	Hibernian	A
10/04/10	Motherwell	H

All fixtures are subject to change.

Post-split fixtures will be announced at a later date.

THE Celtic End at Hampden was awash with green and white as Republic of Ireland duo Darren O'Dea and Aiden McGeady gave the Hoops a 2-0 win over Rangers in the Co-operative Insurance Cup final.

That was Celtic's 14th League Cup final success since their first win back in season 1956/57, and we take a look back at some of the many highlights.

FOURTEEN FANTASTIC FINALS

1 1956/57 Celtic 3 Partick Thistle 0
(after 0-0 draw) (McPhail 2, Mochan)

2 1957/58 Celtic 7 Rangers 1
(McPhail 3, Mochan 2, Wilson, Fernie pen)

3 1965/66 Celtic 2 Rangers 1
(Hughes 2 pens)

4 1966/67 Celtic 1 Rangers 0
(Lennox)

5 1967/68 Celtic 5 Dundee 3
(Chalmers 2, Lennox, Hughes, Wallace)

6 1968/69 Celtic 6 Hibernian 2
(Lennox 3, Craig, Auld, Wallace)

7 1969/70 Celtic 1 St Johnstone 0
(Auld)

8 1974/75 Celtic 6 Hibernian 3
(Deans 3, Johnstone, Murray)

9 1982/83 Celtic 2 Rangers 1
(Nicholas, MacLeod)

10 1997/98 Celtic 3 Dundee United 0
(Rieper, Larsson, Burley)

11 1999/00 Celtic 2 Aberdeen 0
(Riseth, Johnson)

12 2000/01 Celtic 3 Kilmarnock 0
(Larsson 3)

13 2005/06 Celtic 3 Dunfermline 0
(Zurawski, Maloney, Dublin)

14 2008/09 Celtic 2 Rangers 0
(O'Dea, McGeady)

FOURTEEN FANTASTIC FINAL FACTS

In FIVE of the finals, Celtic have beaten Rangers and the 1957/58 7-1 win over the Ibrox side is a record score for a domestic cup final.

Jock Stein led the Celts to six victories while Jimmy McGrory and Gordon Strachan managed two. Billy McNeill, Wim Jansen, Kenny Dalglish and Martin O'Neill all had one win each as manager.

In the 14 finals, Celtic have scored 45 goals for the loss of only 11.

Wim Jansen, Kenny Dalglish, Martin O'Neill and Gordon Strachan all won their first Celtic trophy as manager in these finals.

Celtic have kept clean sheets in the five most recent finals and shut the doors in eight in total.

Billy McPhail, Willie Wallace and Bertie Auld have all scored in two consecutive finals while Bobby Lennox scored in three successive finals.

Billy McNeill played in SIX winning finals in all and he was the only man to both captain AND manage the Celts in winning the trophy.

Billy McPhail, Bobby Lennox, Dixie Deans and Henrik Larsson have all scored hat-tricks in the finals.

No fewer than 25 Celts have scored in the 14 finals: 17 Scots, two Irish, two English, and one each from Denmark, Sweden, Norway and Poland. Only Hibs with five goals and Rangers and Dundee with three scored against the Celts.

Celtic won FIVE consecutive finals between seasons 1965/66 and 1969/70.

Top of the keepers are Ronnie Simpson and Jonathan Gould with three winning appearances each with Gould keeping three clean sheets.

Billy McNeill and Bobby Murdoch played in all FIVE of those consecutive final wins.

Billy McPhail and Bobby Lennox are top scorers in these finals with five goals each while Henrik Larsson scored four.

The total attendance at these finals is 945,211 with the biggest crowd being the 107,609 for the 1965/66 2-1 win over Rangers.

HERE COME THE GHIRLS

THE Celtic Girls' Youth Academy and Celtic Ladies FC continues to go from strength to strength, with squads now running from U11 to U17 in addition to two senior teams.

Underpinning the Youth Academy is a grassroots programme that is open to girls of all abilities providing more young girls with the opportunity to access football, have fun, and benefit from our coaching and learn about the benefits of a healthy lifestyle.

The development programme focuses on the following areas;

* Lifestyle management   * Fitness

* Technique   * Tactics

All of the youth squads excluding the U11s (developmental league undefeated) finished their leagues in December 2008, and all claimed the title of champions in a clean sweep for the club.

Both of the senior squads also made excellent progress although failing to win any trophies with the first team missing out on the title by only three points.

The first team played 25 games in all competitions and won 19 of them, drew twice and lost four while scoring 102 goals for the loss of only 27.

The B team, having just been promoted the previous season as champions of Division Two and fielding many of that term's U17s, played 27 games in all competitions, winning 18 while just losing out in the League Cup final and being knocked out of the Scottish Cup on penalties.

In the Girls' Youth Academy, the U17s claimed the championship in a campaign that saw them win all but one of their matches with many of the players also performing on occasion for the B team and the first team.

These girls are constantly improving which indicates a strong future for Celtic Ladies as a whole.

The U15s didn't have the best of starts to the season but they certainly made up for it in a thrilling finale by claiming the title in fine style.

They lost their first game but never tasted defeat in the league again during the season and clinched the championship in their final league match against Kilmarnock at Lennoxtown.

The girls also won the Friendship Trophy by beating Belfast side Linfield and lifted the Scottish Cup before narrowly missing out on the UK Cup by losing on penalties to Manchester City in the final at Bolton's Reebok Stadium.

The U14s won their mini-season from August to November by winning ALL 14 of their games while scoring an amazing 208 goals for the loss of only one with many of the players still eligible to play at U13 level.

The U13s have also had a remarkable season with many high-scoring games despite the fact that the majority of the girls were still eligible to play at U11 level.

The Celtic Girls' Youth Academy and Celtic Ladies FC would like to acknowledge and thank their sponsors, Glasgow City Building, Clydesdale Bank, Sportsmatch and Nike for their support during season 2008/09:

Check out the Celtic Player Pathway to find out where it could lead you.

To find out more about Celtic Ladies and the training programmes contact Karen on: 0141 551 4332 – 9am to 5pm (Mon to Fri), email kmcinally@celticfc.co.uk

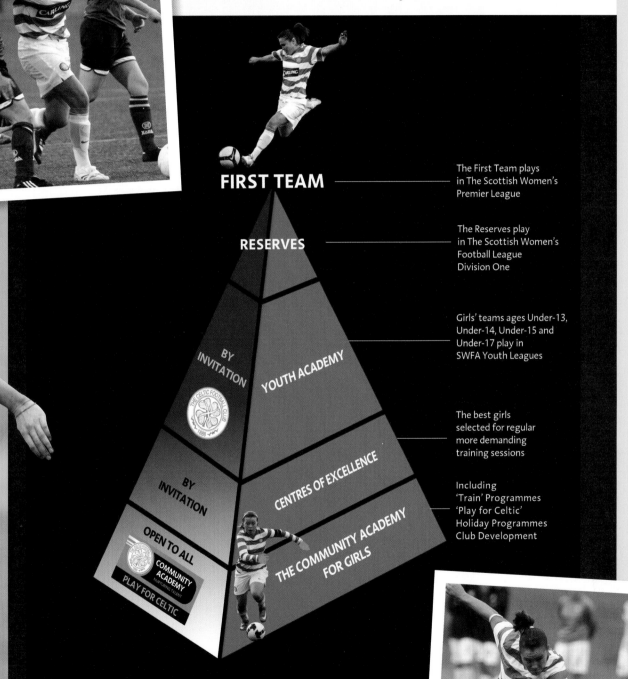

FIRST TEAM — The First Team plays in The Scottish Women's Premier League

RESERVES — The Reserves play in The Scottish Women's Football League Division One

BY INVITATION

YOUTH ACADEMY — Girls' teams ages Under-13, Under-14, Under-15 and Under-17 play in SWFA Youth Leagues

BY INVITATION

CENTRES OF EXCELLENCE — The best girls selected for regular more demanding training sessions

OPEN TO ALL

COMMUNITY ACADEMY NURTURING TALENT
PLAY FOR CELTIC

THE COMMUNITY ACADEMY FOR GIRLS — Including 'Train' Programmes 'Play for Celtic' Holiday Programmes Club Development

The Celtic Community Academy for Girls

PLAYER PATHWAY

CELTIC SOCCER SKOOL

HERE we have the second lesson from some of the best teachers around as they give expert advice on how to become the best footballer you can be.

SCOTT BROWN

TRY and get out as much as possible, get over to the park with your mates or out in the back garden and play football whenever you can. If your mates aren't around, go out and try and work on your weaknesses and improve the things you aren't good at, like using your weaker foot. Try and work on your bad foot, put in crosses, take shots, play passes and you will see improvements. Take advice from people and if you are lucky enough to get the chance to work with older professionals, learn as much from them as you can. But the important thing is to have fun and enjoy your football while you are learning.

PAUL ELLIOTT

I WOULD say to any young player looking to make his way in the game that they should follow their dream, be positive, but prepare for life after football while you are enjoying football. That means getting an education, because if you come out the game in your 30s, if you are lucky enough to play that long, even if you are a multi-millionaire, you will still hopefully have another 40 years ahead of you. So you need your education to protect your money and open up doors within media and business. Follow your dream, enjoy your football, but prepare for life afterwards along the way because your playing career will be like a click of your fingers, it comes and goes.

DARREN O'DEA

THE one thing that every player will tell you is that you have to work hard. You have to constantly try and improve your game, learn and become a better player. There will also be highs and lows and it's important that you don't get too high when there are good times or too low when things aren't going as well for you. Play all the time and make sure you play for fun and enjoy it, but work very hard on improving both feet - that's one of the biggest assets you can have as a player.

BILLY McNEILL

IF I could give advice to a young player trying to make the breakthrough at Celtic Park it would be to listen to the advice that you get from the coaches and senior players. Take every piece of advice on board and don't get carried away with yourself. Enjoy your work, but never think of yourself as being better than anybody else.

SHAUN MALONEY

YOU should have no regrets as a player and try and give it your all. You have to try and improve as much as you can and if you do that, you won't have any regrets or worry about what might have been. You have to listen to your coaches, but it's important that you try and do as much extra training as you can, to be the best player that you can be. If you do work hard you will see results in matches.

THE crowd were in raptures at this stargazing extravaganza as a host of Hoops from the recent past gathered to pay homage to Celtic legend Tommy Burns in a Tribute Match organised to celebrate his life.

The truly nostalgic squad had been put together for the match as Celtic greats lined up to pay tribute to their former team-mate, manager, mentor and friend.

Also included in the Tommy Burns Select, managed by Billy McNeill and Paul McStay, was Tommy's son Jonathan Burns along with Stephen Melville, a supporter who paid £20,000 in a charity auction for the privilege of playing and 14-year-old Islam Feruz representing the Celtic Youth Academy that Tommy masterminded.

It was a fitting and touching occasion, but it was one of happiness in memory of Tommy and one in which, as usual when Tommy Burns was involved, the fans were the winners as they witnessed two teams playing in the TB style and lapped up no fewer than 15 goals.

The final score was 11-4 to the Celtic first-team with much-needed funds going to the three beneficiaries, the Burns family, the Tommy Burns Skin Cancer Trust and the Celtic Charity Fund.

But more importantly, everyone enjoyed a celebration of the life of a true Celtic legend.

Tommy Burns Tribute Match

Sunday, May 31, 2009
Celtic Park, Glasgow

CELTIC...11

(Caldwell 5, 43, McDonald 8, 21, Vennegoor of Hesselink 31, McGeady 49, Donati 53, Ferry 57, Naylor 73, 83, 87)

TOMMY BURNS SELECT...4

(Cadete 14, Keane 17, Hartson 75, Walker 84)

CELTIC

(4-3-3): Brown; Flood, Caldwell, O'Dea, Naylor; Donati, Crosas, Maloney; Vennegoor of Hesselink (Ferry 46), McDonald, Samaras (McGeady 46).

TOMMY BURNS SELECT

(4-4-2): Bonner (Kerr 37); Boyd (Vata 30, Callaghan 72), MacKay (Stubbs 44), Whyte (Baillie 44), McKinlay (Donnelly 60); Burns (Grant 25, Melville 72), Keane (Lambert 25, Feruz 61), MacLeod (Johnson 34, Burns 87), Di Canio (Miller 34, McCluskey 61, Lennon 72); Cadete (Walker 54), van Hooijdonk (Hartson 54).

PUZZLE PAGES

COLOUR ME IN!

Midfielder Scott Brown is about to fire in a thunderbolt shot here and we want you to get out your crayons, ink markers or paints and bring this image to full Celtic technicolour.

GUESS WHO

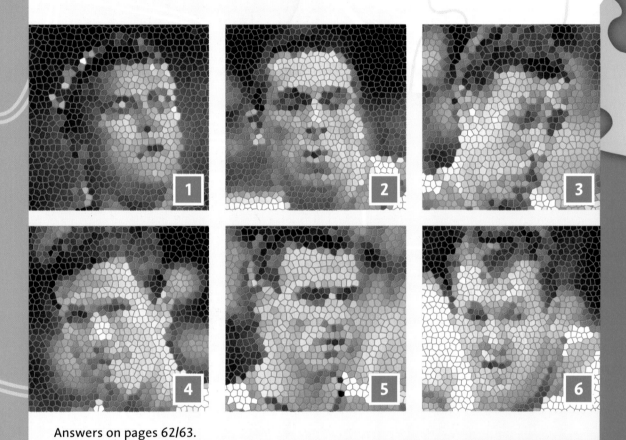

1
2
3
4
5
6

Answers on pages 62/63.

DID YOU KNOW?

Shunsuke Nakamura made headlines around the world when he scored against Manchester United, but did you know that despite his four seasons in Scottish football he scored more goals against the Old Trafford side than he did in games against Dunfermline, Falkirk, Hearts, Inverness CT, Livingston, Motherwell, Stirling Albion, Hibernian, Dundee, Dumbarton, St Johnstone and Clyde!

HOOPS'

HOTSPOTS

HERE we have the second part of the look at where the players like to jet off to when the season has ended.

DARREN O'DEA

First: The first holiday I can really remember was in Portugal with my Mum and Dad. I am an only child, so it was just the three of us, but back then I was young enough and bold enough to go out and make friends and I hung about with other kids on the beach.

Best: That was last year at the Sandy Lane in Barbados. It's one of the best hotels in the world and was absolutely lovely. I don't think I'll ever find better.

Most Recent: You only really get away on holiday during the close season, but I did manage to get a short break for four days in London. I love it there, there was loads of shopping to be done and I went to some nice restaurants.

GEORGIOS SAMARAS

First: Back home in Crete, where I am from, there are some beautiful islands nearby and we would also go to Greece. There are a lot of islands to visit and until I was around 14 or 15 I would go with my Mum and Dad and my family. After that I went with my friends.

Best: I still love to go with my family and friends to visit the islands and I love going back home. We go on a boat and spend a couple of days on each island and it's really nice.

Most Recent: I managed to get away to Paris on one of our free weekends. It's rare to get some time off during the season, but when we do I try and make the most of it. Paris was beautiful, it's a great city to visit and the next city I want to visit is Rome.

SHAUN MALONEY

First: I can't really remember it very well, but the earliest holidays that I can remember were Jersey and Guernsey. We went there for a week, but my first lads' holiday was when I joined Celtic and we all went to Magaluf when I was about 17. It was an experience!

Best Holiday: Recently, it was the whole of my family going away to Portugal. I liked that a lot because during the season I don't really get the chance to see much of anyone, so it was great. The weather was a bonus and the people are lovely in Portugal, but I really loved getting the chance to see all my family.

Most Recent: I went over to Dubai for five nights recently and it was nice enough and really good to get a break. I enjoyed it, but I don't think I'll be back. I have been once and I like going on holiday to different places each year and trying to see as much of the world as possible.

AIDEN McGEADY

First Holiday: The first holiday I can remember is going to Greece when I was about three or four. I went with my Mum and Dad and my sister, my brother wasn't born then. As I got older I would go and make friends, but when I went on holiday I always had a football with me and my Dad and I would go out and play football a lot.

Best: I went to Cancun with my friends last year and that was brilliant, but the best holiday I had was probably in Malia, the year before that.

Most Recent: I went to Dubai with my girlfriend and that was great. It was really hot, there was plenty to do and we were in a nice hotel, so I really enjoyed it. Everything was good about it.

KOKI MIZUNO

First: We used to go on holiday in Japan to different places. I had never actually been abroad until a few years ago. My brothers all played football, so it was rare for us to get together as a family and go places, it was a treat whenever we were together.

Best: I went to Hawaii two years ago with my wife and that was the first time I had been abroad. I loved it, it was a very beautiful island.

Most Recent: Now that I live in Scotland I enjoy going back home to Japan on holiday. It's important to try and get home as often as possible, but during the season it can be difficult because we are so busy.

GR-EIGHT STUFF

CELTIC'S reserve side are now looking for one over the eight after last season's championship-winning campaign was their eighth in a row.

The Young Hoops made sure of their eighth successive title in the best possible way by recording a 1-0 win over Rangers at Ibrox when their opponents were their closest rivals and still in with a shout of the title themselves.

However, a Simon Ferry goal in the 70th minute proved to be the only counter of the day and number eight was in the bag as the Celtic fans, who outnumbered the home fans, made their presence felt throughout the game.

Eight days later, the second string welcomed

Dundee United to Celtic Park for their final game of the campaign and rounded off the season in style with a 4-0 win before being presented with the trophy.

The eight-in-a-row run started away back in season 2001/02 when Livingston, a full 13 points away were the nearest challengers and the closest the second-placed team has been was in season 2005/06 when Rangers finished four points behind.

The biggest points gap during the eight-in-a-row was in season 2006/07 when the Young Hoops finished a full 22 points ahead of Motherwell.

Coach Willie McStay said after the Ibrox win: *"To win eight titles is fantastic. Personally, I'm very proud but there are so many people who have played their part. The boys have all worked hard and I'm delighted for Danny McGrain, who also works extremely hard with them.*

"Most importantly, it was for the players. If one player from this performance can go and make it in the first-team, then our job is done. Hopefully, the players have shown they aren't that far away.

"This was a stage for the boys. They had to go out and show the management and coaching staff that they could do it in a game like this at Ibrox."

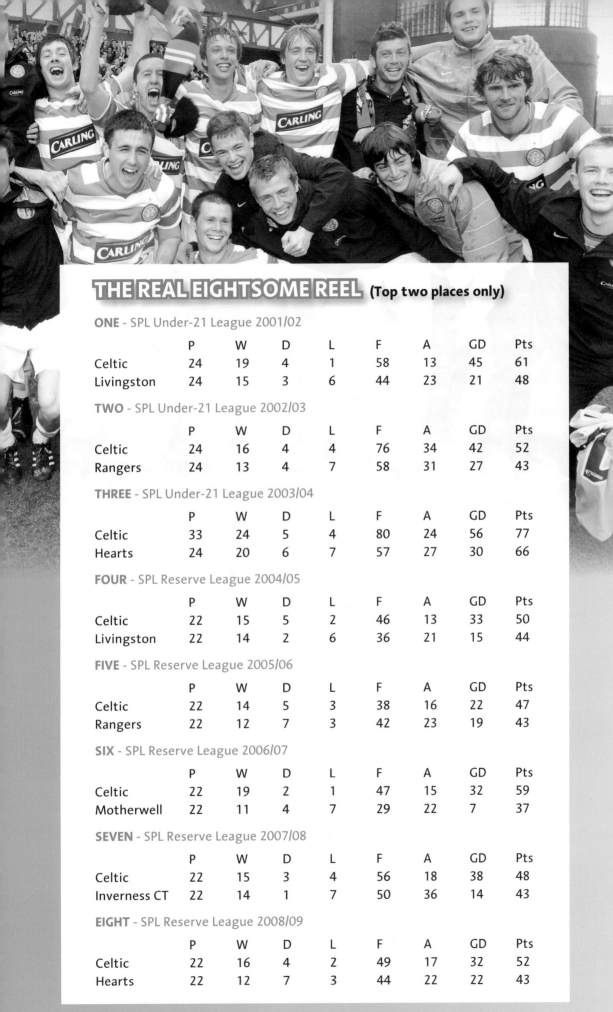

THE REAL EIGHTSOME REEL (Top two places only)

ONE - SPL Under-21 League 2001/02

	P	W	D	L	F	A	GD	Pts
Celtic	24	19	4	1	58	13	45	61
Livingston	24	15	3	6	44	23	21	48

TWO - SPL Under-21 League 2002/03

	P	W	D	L	F	A	GD	Pts
Celtic	24	16	4	4	76	34	42	52
Rangers	24	13	4	7	58	31	27	43

THREE - SPL Under-21 League 2003/04

	P	W	D	L	F	A	GD	Pts
Celtic	33	24	5	4	80	24	56	77
Hearts	24	20	6	7	57	27	30	66

FOUR - SPL Reserve League 2004/05

	P	W	D	L	F	A	GD	Pts
Celtic	22	15	5	2	46	13	33	50
Livingston	22	14	2	6	36	21	15	44

FIVE - SPL Reserve League 2005/06

	P	W	D	L	F	A	GD	Pts
Celtic	22	14	5	3	38	16	22	47
Rangers	22	12	7	3	42	23	19	43

SIX - SPL Reserve League 2006/07

	P	W	D	L	F	A	GD	Pts
Celtic	22	19	2	1	47	15	32	59
Motherwell	22	11	4	7	29	22	7	37

SEVEN - SPL Reserve League 2007/08

	P	W	D	L	F	A	GD	Pts
Celtic	22	15	3	4	56	18	38	48
Inverness CT	22	14	1	7	50	36	14	43

EIGHT - SPL Reserve League 2008/09

	P	W	D	L	F	A	GD	Pts
Celtic	22	16	4	2	49	17	32	52
Hearts	22	12	7	3	44	22	22	43

CELTIC ACADEMY

PLAY FOR CELTIC IN THE CELTIC COMMUNITY ACADEMY

THE Celtic Community Academy's player progress pathway is a clearly defined route for youngsters to be selected for the elite Celtic Youth Academy which has teams from under-11 to under-19.

Players from 5 year of age to senior now have a fantastic opportunity to get a foot on the ladder, as well as an opportunity to play regular matches against other clubs in local associations throughout Scotland.

If during training and in the games a player shows potential, he'll be invited to join a Centre of Excellence (depending on age). . . and who knows? The next step could be an invitation to join one of our seven Development Centres situated across the country.

HOW IT WORKS

There are two options provided:

Option 1: Train Only Centres

For boys aged 5 - 13 there is an opportunity to receive a coaching only programme with our talented Celtic Community Academy coaching staff. This programme is designed for young players who enjoy meeting new friends and having fun whilst developing their football skills. The aim of the Community Academy training programme is to provide an opportunity for young players regardless of ability to "Train and Play the Celtic Way". Players will train at their local centre and also receive information and advice on diet and nutrition.

Option 2: Play for Celtic

The Play for Celtic programme is the ultimate football experience for young players and adults! The players will train as a squad (U8 - Senior) at their local centre. All players will receive full Nike training kit and then at the weekend pull on the world famous green and white hoops and represent Celtic against local clubs in the Scottish Youth Football Association (SYFA) affiliated associations and Scottish Amateur Football Association (SAFA).

Centre of Excellence Programme

The very best of players within the Community Academy will be invited to join a Centre of Excellence for six week cycles. During this time they will receive very careful attention and will play in matches against Celtic Youth Academy teams or other teams of appropriate age and ability. They will also be advised to continue training and playing with their own centre/squad.

At their weekly training sessions, an even greater demand will be placed on the players with regard to technique, tactical nous and fitness. Education in sport science and diet, practice in speed, agility and quickness will be stepped up.

The players will have a self-assessment book and written feedback to the players and their parents will be provided at the end of each cycle for discussion at a parents' night.

Extended Player Pathway

Study the pathway and you'll see some of the routes to becoming an established first-team player at Celtic.

For further information contact Hazel Wilson: email: hwilson@celticfc.co.uk
tel: 0871 226 1888 (option 5) or 0141 551 4321 (Monday to Friday 9.30 am to 5 pm)

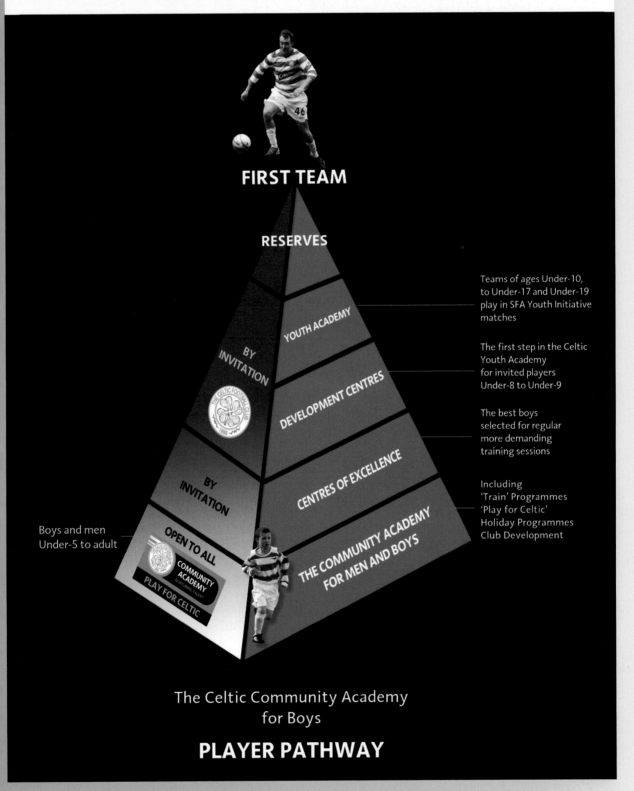

FIRST TEAM

RESERVES

YOUTH ACADEMY

Teams of ages Under-10, to Under-17 and Under-19 play in SFA Youth Initiative matches

BY INVITATION

DEVELOPMENT CENTRES

The first step in the Celtic Youth Academy for invited players Under-8 to Under-9

The best boys selected for regular more demanding training sessions

BY INVITATION

CENTRES OF EXCELLENCE

Including 'Train' Programmes 'Play for Celtic' Holiday Programmes Club Development

Boys and men Under-5 to adult

OPEN TO ALL

COMMUNITY ACADEMY

PLAY FOR CELTIC

THE COMMUNITY ACADEMY FOR MEN AND BOYS

The Celtic Community Academy for Boys

PLAYER PATHWAY

PUZZLE PAGES

DOT-TO-DOT

Join up all of the dots in this picture and see if you can identify this well-known Celtic character who always plays his part in every home game.

*Indicates new line start (Answer on pages 62/63)

FIRST SENIOR CLUBS

Here is a list of famous Celtic names past and present, but do you know who their first senior teams were?

01   Gary Caldwell

02   Willie Wallace

03   Andreas Hinkel

04   Barry Robson

05   Glenn Loovens

06   Brian McClair

07   Frank McAvennie

08   Davie Provan

09   Roy Keane

10   Billy McNeill

The answers are on pages 62/63

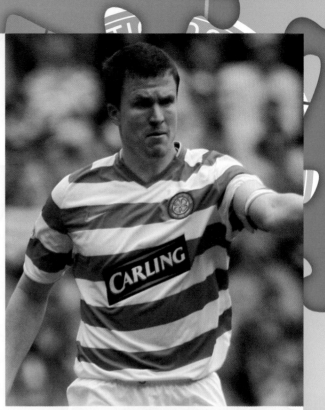

DID YOU KNOW?

Kelly is the most frequently seen surname in Celtic team-sheets down through the decades. There have been 10 Kellys in all to play for the first team: Charlie Kelly (1891), Charlie Kelly (1944-45), Frank Kelly (1918), Frank Kelly (1943-47), Jimmy Kelly (1888-97), John Kelly (1929-30), Johnny Kelly (1938-41), John Kelly (1939-40), Johnny Kelly (1960-62) and Paddy Kelly (1995-97).

SCIENCE FACTION

YOU'LL have seen the players in the warm-up before matches, going through their final drills on the pitch, but the real work is done behind the scenes at Lennoxtown.

Sports Science has become a key part of the day-to-day routine at Celtic and has been credited by a number of the players as having made real improvements to their game.

Aiden McGeady, Darren O'Dea and Gary Caldwell are three who speak regularly about the importance of Sports Science, with training plans improving their strength, speed and stamina.

Just as vital is what a player does after the final whistle and there are a few simple rules you can follow that will help you improve your game and all-round fitness – as well as giving you the edge over your opponent.

Here are just a few of the ways that the Celtic players prepare for matches that you can learn from.

ENDURANCE

By preparing well and improving your endurance you will be able to compete at a high level for the whole game, whether that's 90 or 120 minutes. Many decisive goals are scored in the last 15 minutes when players are tired and you will also be able to exhaust your opponent by running quicker and further than them. With good endurance you will also be able to recover better and play more matches – at Celtic some players play more than 50 games a season.

STRENGTH

Strength is crucial in building confidence and if you work hard in training and improve it, you will be able to protect your body, keep the ball in a one-on-one challenge and keep your opponent at a safe distance. You will also find that it is easier to prevent injury, while some training methods can also improve your power and speed, allowing you to change pace. Listen to your coaches, work hard and you will see the benefits.

REST AND RECOVERY

Recovery is a very important part of every player's preparation for matches and when you are young and still growing it is crucial. The harder you train and work, the more tired you will become, and this will affect your fitness and concentration in matches. Every footballer has to get plenty sleep, which means getting to bed early!

FOOD

By eating the proper diet, players can train hard, reduce the risk of illness and injury and do their best in matches. At Lennoxtown their meals include plenty of vegetables, fruits, beans, cereals, lean meats, fish, chicken and dairy foods. Between three and five hours before a game they have their main meal, with many players having pasta with chicken, or if it's a midday kick-off, a big bowl of porridge or cereal, some fruit and orange juice. Some then have a cereal bar or fruit an hour before the game as well. It's also important to eat healthily all through the week.

FLUIDS

Every Celtic player is careful to avoid dehydration and takes in plenty of fluids throughout the day. All of them have milk, water and fruit juice with meals and drink water and energy drinks before and after training. But when you are growing up, some energy drinks might not be right for you and it may be best to avoid or dilute them. During matches you'll also see the players having a mouthful of water, even on a cold day when you may not be thirsty - because you'll always get dehydrated. Dehydration is also one of the causes of cramp.

AFTER THE FINAL WHISTLE

The period after a match is called 'The Golden Hour' and this is the most important time to top up your stores of energy. If the players even wait for two hours before having food and water it has a huge impact on their recovery. At the end of a match, sometimes on the team coach or plane back home to Glasgow, they will drink plenty of water, have a sandwich, a yoghurt and either a cereal or chocolate bar. Then, ideally within three hours of the final whistle, they have a meal including bread, pasta, rice, potatoes, fruit juice and yoghurt.

WARMING UP AND COOLING DOWN

It's important to warm up and, if possible, cool down after a match. This is crucial in preparing for games and can help avoid injury afterwards. If you are a substitute you have to be ready to come on and make an impact at any time and you will see the players doing stretches and light exercises during intervals at Celtic Park. Even at half time the players start to warm up five minutes before the start of the second half.

HERE we have the second part of the look at some of the players who inspired your Celtic heroes when they were younger.

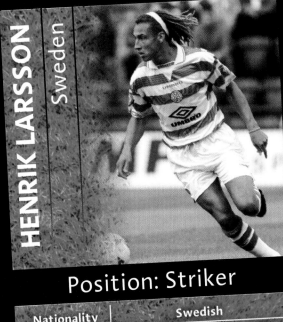

HENRIK LARSSON
Sweden

Position: Striker

Nationality	Swedish
Former Clubs	Feyenoord, Celtic, Barcelona, Manchester United
Notable Achievement	One of the Greatest Ever Celts, Henrik gave his best years to Celtic and then went on to win a Spanish title and Champions League with Barcelona.

SHAUN MALONEY

"When I first joined the club I was 16 and my favourite player was Henrik Larsson. It was amazing to get the chance to work with him at Celtic, and not only is he one of the club's great players, he's one of the greatest players of this recent era. Before that, my old man was a bit of an Arsenal fan and Dennis Bergkamp was one of the players I liked to watch. I was a big fan of his when I was younger, he was a spectacular player, but up here it was Henrik."

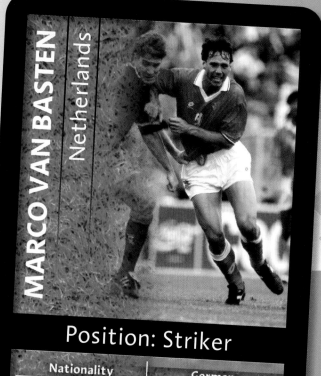

MARCO VAN BASTEN
Netherlands

Position: Striker

Nationality	German
Former Clubs	Ajax, AC Milan
Notable Achievement	Three time European Player of the Year and a former World Player of the Year.

GEORGIOS SAMARAS

"I loved to watch Marco van Basten, he was one of the great footballers. You should try and watch some of his matches if you ever get the chance – he was the complete striker. When I was growing up I had another hero, but he wasn't a footballer and I used to be crazy about the basketball player, Michael Jordan. My Father allowed me to get up at three or four o'clock in the morning and watch when he had a big game on. I would then go into school the next day and ask people if they had seen the game – but no one else ever watched them! But van Basten was my football hero and it was a shame he was forced to finish his career early because of injury."

KOKI MIZUNO

"When I was growing up my favourite player was Kazu, he was a very famous player in Japan and still is. Everybody loved him and when I was at nursery school everyone had his boots with his signature on them. Everybody wanted to play like him and have the career that he had, playing in so many different countries, he was everyone's hero."

PAOLO DI CANIO
Italy

Position: Striker

Nationality	Italian
Former Clubs	Lazio, Juventus, AC Milan, Celtic, Sheffield Wednesday, West Ham
Notable Achievement	Won FIFA Fair Play award for 'good sportsmanship' for refusing to score when the opposing keeper was down injured.

KAZUYOSHI MIURA
Japan

Position: Midfielder/Striker

Nationality	Japanese
Former Clubs	Santos, Palmeiras, Verdy Kawasaki, Genoa, Dynamo Zagreb, Yokohama
Notable Achievement	Still playing at the age of 42, Kazu first left Japan at 15 years of age to play for Santos in Brazil.

AIDEN McGEADY

"When I was young it was Paolo Di Canio. He was the one that every young Celtic supporter looked up to. He was only here for about a year, but he made an impact. After that, it was Henrik Larsson. I loved Henrik and Lubomir Moravcik as well and Lubo was my kind of player – he would get on the ball and beat people and he was unbelievably gifted. I got the chance to work with Henrik and it's incredible to think that I made my debut alongside him and I actually played up front that day as well. Strangely enough, Lubo's son used to play for the Celtic team below me. Lubo would come along on a Friday night and train with them and sometimes join in with us."

DIEGO MARADONA
Argentina

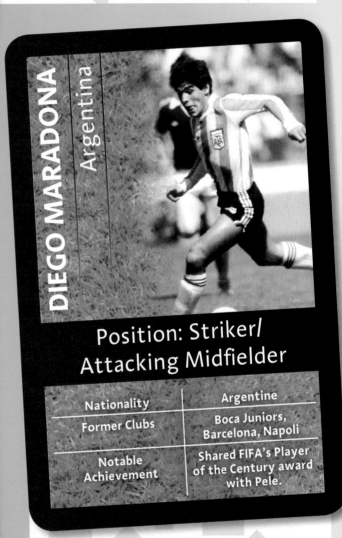

Position: Striker/ Attacking Midfielder

Nationality	Argentine
Former Clubs	Boca Juniors, Barcelona, Napoli
Notable Achievement	Shared FIFA's Player of the Century award with Pele.

SCOTT BROWN

"Maradona was frightening, he's the best player I have ever seen. He would happily take players on and just go by them, and he practically won Napoli the Italian league single-handedly. He was also great to watch at the World Cup and his goal against England just made it for me – he goes past the entire team before scoring! Brilliant! He is easily my favourite player."

PARADISE TREASURE HUNT
PARADISE TREASURE HUNT
PARADISE TREASURE HUNT
PARADISE TREASURE HUNT
PARADISE TREASURE HUNT
PARADISE TREASURE HUNT

GRASPING THE MEDAL

HOOPS stars Gary Caldwell, Stephen McManus, Scott Brown, Paul Hartley and Shaun Maloney all featured when Scotland entertained Argentina at Hampden during the season just past, but it was a Celtic Under-14 player who grabbed all the limelight that week.

Diego Maradona's superstars trained at Celtic Park two nights before the game and it was young Adam Brown who came to the rescue when Real Madrid's Fernando Gago lost a gold medallion from his neck during training.

The Celtic Under-14s helped the superstar sweep the turf following the training session and Adam spotted the trinket near the centre-circle.

Maradona rewarded the Celtic youngster by handing him his hat and gloves and lifting him into the air.

Adam said: "Along with my team-mates from the Celtic Under-14s, I'd been asked to be a ballboy for the Argentina training.

"Gago, the Argentina midfielder, chested the ball during training and his medal fell on to the pitch. They asked us to help search for it and I actually swapped places with someone in the line.

"A few seconds later, I found it and Maradona came over to me. He said 'Thanks, thanks very much' and then lifted me up. He gave me his gloves and his hat. I'm going to put them in a frame.

"It's a dream come true to meet Maradona. I never thought I'd ever get the chance. He's one of my football heroes. He's one of the best players ever to play the game."

The Cumbernauld Bhoy's dad Fraser was in the stand at Celtic Park, but his mum Pauline was at home oblivious to the fact that her son was making headlines around the world.

She said: "My husband texted me to say that Adam had been on the pitch with Maradona and that he'd been interviewed.

"I switched on the TV and I was glued to the sports channel for about two hours. I just couldn't believe it when I saw Adam being lifted up on the pitch.

"We saw his picture on the Celtic website, but we didn't realise how big a story it would be. When we bought the newspapers the next morning, we couldn't believe it.

"It's just unbelievable. One minute, he's asked to be a ballboy and the next minute he's all over the news with one of the most famous footballers ever. It was an incredible 24 hours."

SPOT THE DIFFERENCE (Page 22)

ANSWERS

SPL SEASON 2008/09 QUIZ ANSWERS (Page 23)

01 Marc Crosas and Glenn Loovens.

02 It was his 'second debut' after re-signing with the club.

03 Willo Flood.

04 New Douglas Park and New St Mirren Park.

05 The Hoops beat St Mirren 7-0.

06 Scott Cuthbert (St Mirren), Paul Caddis (Dundee United), Cillian Sheridan (Motherwell) and Paul McGowan (Hamilton).

07 Gary Caldwell and Scott Brown with 36 appearances each.

08 Chris Killen.

09 Seventeen.

10 The St Mirren defender scored Celtic's only own goal of the term.

WORDSEARCH ANSWERS (Page 27)

01 ScottMcDonald

02 Barrowfield

03 International

04 Japan

05 Lions

06 LiamBrady

07 Pylons

08 Hoops

09 LeagueCup

K	R	N	N	Y	K	R	M	C	E	Z	B	C
S	C	O	T	T	M	C	D	O	N	A	L	D
O	N	A	R	E	V	N	I	K	R	D	S	L
U	A	L	R	B	T	D	J	R	F	N	T	Y
P	P	P	N	A	A	S	O	T	O	N	X	D
U	A	L	B	N	D	W	K	L	K	H	O	A
C	J	X	L	T	F	I	Y	C	K	L	N	R
E	L	A	G	I	R	P	S	X	O	J	N	B
U	T	Z	E	R	O	N	C	E	H	J	E	M
G	T	L	J	T	W	N	L	Y	V	Y	L	A
A	D	N	O	I	P	M	S	H	C	T	L	I
E	P	U	C	N	A	E	S	P	O	O	H	L
L	A	N	O	I	T	A	N	R	E	T	N	I